Leaders, Legends, & Legacies:

Jackson Kelly's Bicentennial History

2022

Compiled by Stephen R. Crislip and Joshua A. Claybourn, with editorial support from Sherry B. Darrell.

First Printing: 2022

ISBN 978-1-387-43041-3

Jackson Kelly PLLC
P.O. Box 553
Charleston, WV 25322

The Jackson Kelly Legacy

1822: Benjamin H. Smith

1865: Smith & Knight

1884: Knight & Couch

1892: Brown, Jackson & Knight

1947: Jackson, Kelly, Morrison & Moxley

1953: Jackson, Kelly, Holt & Moxley

1956: Jackson, Kelly, Holt & O'Farrell

1998: Jackson & Kelly

1999: Jackson & Kelly PLLC

2002: Jackson Kelly PLLC

Contents

Dedication

We dedicate this book, first, to our clients,
the heart of Jackson Kelly's efforts.

We dedicate this history, too, to Jackson Kelly's team
past and present, whose hard work and talent
has fueled success for two centuries.

Prologue

Since our firm's founding in 1822, Jackson Kelly has grown from a single office in Charleston, West Virginia, to ten offices in Colorado, Indiana, Kentucky, Ohio, Pennsylvania, West Virginia, and the District of Columbia. Throughout its history, Jackson Kelly helped shape the legal profession and its regional and national footprints. Our lawyers have provided astute counsel and representation to clients and served as leaders in our communities and our profession.

Of course, any law firm with roots stretching back 200 years clearly includes visionary leaders who stretched and adapted. Proudly ranking among the oldest law firms in the United States—by one measure, the sixth oldest in the country—we tell our firm's history to spotlight Jackson Kelly's rich culture and to assemble in one place the tales, challenges, and triumphs marking the past 200 years.

Despite changes in our profession, and in our country, we at Jackson Kelly have never changed our focus on clients. Our firm's client relationships do not simply happen—we cultivate and maintain relationships in a way often lost in the "big law" world. We operate as a cohesive unit providing a range of services to our clients, always approaching legal services with attention to detail, promptness, and precision.

As we look to the future, Jackson Kelly will flourish by retaining our core values—vision, adaptability, and client focus. Our enduring success will depend on our ability to attract and retain a highly skilled, diverse team of professionals who will, I am confident, outpace our competitors in service to clients.

Cheers to another 200 years of excellence.

Ellen S. Cappellanti
Managing Member
(2015-2022)

Robert G. Tweel
Managing Member
(beginning 2023)

Benjamin Harrison Smith

Jackson Kelly's story begins with Benjamin Harrison Smith, born in October 1797 in Rockingham County, Virginia, near the heart of Shenandoah Valley southwest of Washington, D.C. Smith's family moved west in 1810 to a farm in Lancaster, Ohio. Among several factors prompting the move, the family wished to settle where they could safely free their slaves. As planned, the Smiths brought several African Americans to Ohio and freed them; some later settled in Lancaster and became "good and useful citizens." Among them was Scipio Smith, who ran a tin and coppersmith trade and became the first black businessman in town.[1]

The move west surely involved hardships. At times the landscape offered thick woods, and even near farmlands the caravan routes were often rugged and undeveloped. Nevertheless, one traveler described Lancaster at this period as "a handsome little town" with "about 100 homes." Newspapers advertised businesses opening frequently, including the Lancaster (Ohio) Bank, the town's first financial institution, in 1816.[2]

As a boy in Virginia, young Benjamin Smith studied three years "in the English branches only," which meant he took courses in speaking and writing.[3] But once in Ohio, he attended school only briefly before

---

[1] He later renamed himself "Scipio Africanus," the same name of one of Rome's best and well-known generals and statesmen. Contosta, *Lancaster, Ohio, 1800-2000*, 16 and 67.

[2] Contosta, 18.

[3] Benjamin Smith began his schooling in Harrisonburg, a short distance from the family home. He studied for three years under Mr. Clark, "who instructed in the English branches only." Contosta, 20.

devoting himself to farm work from 1812 to 1815. A knee injury, though, confined him to bed for several weeks and forever altered his life—as well as our firm's. While nursing his injury, Smith picked up a book titled *Thinks I to Myself*, which he devoured. Hooked on reading, Smith requested more books from a neighbor and developed a love of reading. But he also realized he needed more tools to appreciate his readings; in particular, he wanted to understand classical allusions. Thus, he sought a formal education.

In the early 1800s, especially west of the Alleghenies, there were few educational institutions. Because colleges were rare, white males from affluent families often traveled to eastern schools or took advantage of one of the few frontier opportunities. Still mostly frontier, Ohio had become a state in 1803, just seven years before Smith's arrival. In 1804, the Ohio General Assembly established a university in Athens which, in 1809, became the first institution of higher learning in the Northwest Territory, beginning in a two-story, two-room, brick structure with just three students.[4]

Though we now refer to the school as Ohio University, at that time most citizens called it the *academy* or, officially, the *Seminary*. Eventually the academy became a preparatory school; completion of a second building in 1818 led Ohioans to call it Ohio University.[5]

Because most frontier students came to the academy with rudimentary education, the coursework did not compare to that in northeastern schools. The academy focused on grammar, arithmetic, Latin, Greek, geography, mathematics, logic, rhetoric, and natural and moral philosophy. Tuition cost a few dollars, primarily to cover

---

[4] Brinkley, Alan, *The Unfinished Nation*, 221.
[5] Hoover, *The History of Ohio University*, 24.

firewood costs. Students were required to "recite six days a week, be examined quarterly by trustees, and appear once a year in public exhibition."[6]

Benjamin Harrison Smith began studying at Ohio Seminary in 1815 as one of about a dozen students. Although some were quite young, under age 12, Smith entered the school at about age 18. When his father died in 1817, he noted in his will Benjamin's "highly advanced intellect" and left an inheritance to pay "necessary and reasonable expenses in finishing and completing (young Benjamin's) education."[7]

Benjamin Harrison Smith remained at Ohio Seminary for four years, graduating in 1819. Thereafter he returned to Lancaster and studied law for two-and-a-half to three years with Thomas Ewing, who had graduated from Ohio Seminary four years earlier as one of the first two students to earn a degree. In 1821, Smith was admitted to practice before the Ohio Supreme Court.

Ewing served as a great mentor for Smith. Ewing worked in the law office of General Philemon Beecher, a leading lawyer in Lancaster and a state legislator. When General Beecher was away at the General Assembly, Ewing led the law practice and built a good reputation for himself—so good, in fact, that he won General Beecher's approval to marry Beecher's daughter. At Ewing's suggestion, Smith chose to practice law in Charleston, then still part of Virginia. After an initial visit, Smith officially moved to Charleston on May 27, 1822, and opened his

---

[6] Hoover, 1-5; 21-41.
[7] Smith, *From the Shenandoah to the Kanawha*, 211 & 216. Benjamin Smith's father left each of his children the equivalent of $1,000, but added the note about expenses for Benjamin to complete his education. Because Benjamin Smith (the elder) was among seven nominated by Bishop Asbury to serve as Trustees of the area's first school in 1794, likely he had some educational foundation.

law office. This date—May 27—marks the official birth of Jackson Kelly.

A Whig (like Smith), Ewing eventually rose to serve as U.S. Senator and later became Secretary of the Treasury under William Henry Harrison and Secretary of the Interior under Zachary Taylor. Though nominated to become Secretary of War under Andrew Johnson, Ewing failed to receive Senate confirmation.[8]

Benjamin Smith's new law practice focused on land titles. A generation or two previously, the Virginia legislature sought to attract settlers by dramatically reducing the price per acre—from $5.80 before 1788 to a mere $0.02 in 1793. That drop caused millions of acres to change hands, often without proper surveys, thereby leading to plenty of land disputes that produced "a profitable living for generations of lawyers."[9]

Benjamin Smith's law practice grew in the Kanawha Valley encompassing Charleston thanks to growing activity in the salt business, timber and mining, river transportation, and construction of flatboats to transport salt. In 1823, he brought 60 lawsuits in the spring term of the local court, at that time the largest docket for any lawyer at the bar.[10]

In 1826, Smith married Roxalana Emmeline Noyes, daughter of Isaac and Cynthia Morris Noyes. Together they had one son, Isaac Noyes Smith, born in 1832, and two daughters. Some of Roxalana's family were lawyers with the firm Brigham & Noyes.

---

[8] Miller, "Thomas Ewing: Last of the Whigs," 1933.
[9] Shaffer, *Clash of Loyalties*, 23.
[10] Atkinson, *History of Kanawha County*, 261.

Beyond the law, and like his mentor, Ewing, Smith achieved success in politics. In 1833, he won election to the Virginia State Senate and re-election in 1835, running in part on a campaign to improve land laws, particularly for lands in (then) western Virginia. Although Smith first declined to run a third time, ultimately he ran successfully again. After accomplishing his goals for land-law reform in 1838, he retired at the end of the first year in that third term. The same year he received an honorary A.M. degree from Ohio University, the equivalent of a master's degree.[11]

For most of his professional life Benjamin Smith carried the title "colonel" although available historical sources do not explain its origin. Some speculate he served in the county militia.

According to George W. Atkinson, an attorney who wrote several publications about West Virginia Bar members and prominent citizens, few lawyers in the state matched Smith's expertise in land laws. For more than 40 years Smith "was actively employed in every land case of importance in the Circuit Court, and in many out of it, most of them being of great complexity, and involving lands of great value."[12] Atkinson added, "In all of the vast number of land cases in which the Colonel has been engaged as an attorney, about nine tenths of them have been decided in favor of his clients. This, of itself, would establish his reputation as a land lawyer."[13]

Others also recognized Smith's expertise. William S. Laidley, a Smith contemporary and historian of Charleston and the Kanawha Valley, viewed the Colonel as the premier land lawyer in the region. John H. Tinney, president of the West Virginia State Bar, wrote of him:

Colonel Smith was able to craft and obtain passages of Constitutional provisions and statutory implementation of a system that not only was just and equitable, but [also] enabled generations of title examiners to approve titles to lands where there were

---

[11] Smith had not received a degree upon graduation 18 years before because the university was not yet authorized by law to confer degrees. Atkinson, 262.

[12] Atkinson, *History of Kanawha County*, 262.

[13] *Ibid.*

conflicting claims. This system provided a jumpstart to the settlement and commercial development of West Virginia. Colonel Smith deserves a lion's share of the credit for our state's development. Moreover, he left a legacy of law that long outlasted him. He truly deserves to be remembered as a West Virginia lawyer-patriot.[14]

This impressive reputation caught the attention of several U.S. presidents. For instance, in 1848 Zachary Taylor appointed Smith District Attorney of the United States for the Western District of Virginia; he remained in office during Millard Fillmore's presidency. But because Smith was a Whig, Franklin Pierce, a Democrat, did not re-appoint him in 1856.

In the 1830s the Whig party emerged as a coalition of National Republicans (from the old Federalist Party), Anti-Roman Catholics, and disgruntled Democrats, all brought together by opposition to President Andrew Jackson's expanded executive powers. In Virginia, Whigs sought to grow business and commerce, particularly through greater federal action. In particular, Whigs supported infrastructure improvements, public education, robust banking, and high tariffs. In Smith's western Virginia, Whigs believed such policies might help their region compete with the more prosperous Piedmont and Shenandoah areas. The first Whig president, William Henry Harrison, was elected in 1840; a second Whig, Zachary Taylor, was elected in 1848. By then, however, the Whig and Democratic parties had grown almost indistinguishable. Moreover, the growing antislavery movement caused both parties to splinter. Eventually the new Republican Party absorbed what Whigs remained during the leadup to the Civil War.

---

[14] *West Virginia Lawyer*, August 2001, 4.

In 1861, Smith was elected to the West Virginia Constitutional Convention and assumed a large role in its proceedings held from 1861 to 1863.[15] He also played a prominent role in dividing the Commonwealth of Virginia. Granville Davisson Hall, official reporter of the constitutional convention, wrote of him:

> The member who appeared most zealous and influential in shaping the action of the Convention in this matter [forfeited and delinquent lands] was Col. Benjamin H. Smith, delegate from Logan. Colonel Smith was a resident of Charleston, and at the time U.S. District Attorney, a lawyer of ability and experience and perhaps more familiar with the subject of Virginia wild lands than any other member of the Convention. He had been permitted to come upon a petition signed by fifteen refugees claiming to be from Logan County, who were at Camp Piatt, the headquarters of the 44th Regiment.
>
> [Although] several other members of the Convention held seats by credentials as slender as these, none of them attempted to exercise such a controlling influence as Colonel Smith. He did not come into the convention until late in the session, and all appearances indicated he had sought admission to a seat only because of his interest in the subject.[16]

In January 1861, the Virginia Legislature adopted resolutions enabling Virginia to act as mediator between the national government and the seceded states. The resolutions called for a convention to deal with secession. Those attending that convention strongly favored

---

[15] Charles H. Ambler lists Smith among "so-called Fathers" of the state in *West Virginia: The Mountain State*.

[16] Maxwell, 13.

preserving the Union—if states' rights could also be preserved. But once Lincoln issued a call for volunteers, which many Virginians perceived as a show of force to compel seceding states back into the Union, the mood at the convention changed; on April 17, 1861, delegates adopted an ordinance of secession to submit to popular vote.

Delegates from many of Virginia's western districts returned home in disgust to the ordinance and opposition to secession; and once home, many of them met to discuss options for helping preserve the Union. At a large meeting in Clarksburg in April 1861, some delegates adopted resolutions recommending that pro-Union counties each send representatives to a convention in Wheeling that May. There, in Wheeling, they formally voted against the secession ordinance and agreed that if Virginia voted to secede, the northwestern counties would appoint delegates to a second convention, to meet in Wheeling in June 1861, to consider breaking away from Virginia.

As expected, Virginia's popular vote held on May 23, 1861, favored secession. The pro-Union Wheeling convention—what most historians refer to as the Second Convention—met in the belief it carried out Virginia's proper governmental duties. Delegates declared void all acts taken by Virginia to secede and declare war against the United States. By resolution, these delegates vacated all state offices; and acting as a reorganized Virginia government, the Second Convention elected Francis H. Pierpont governor and filled other state offices. The new General Assembly met, elected U.S. Senators, and subsequently selected U.S. Representatives, all admitted to Congress and recognized by the national government as the legitimate government of Virginia.

Constituent Convention of Virginia, Assembled in the
Custom-House at Wheeling, Ohio Co., June, 1861

Then the Second Convention recessed until later that fall; in August 1861, it reassembled and passed an ordinance calling for a popular vote for forming a new state and for holding a convention to frame a constitution if the popular vote favored such a new state. Many peculiarities surround this popular vote—the Union army occupied much of the area and prevented Confederate sympathizers from voting, and most pro-statehood votes came from just 16 counties in the northern panhandle. In Wheeling only about a fourth of registered voters cast votes. According to the official tally, new statehood garnered 18,408 votes in favor and 781 votes against.[17]

Despite some questions and controversies about the legitimacy of that statehood vote, delegates met in November 1861 to write a new state constitution to submit to popular vote in April 1862. According to George W. Atkinson, who later served as governor of West Virginia, Smith, a long-time and outspoken Union defender, did more than anyone else in the Kanawha Valley to prevent Virginia from seceding and remained a staunch Union supporter throughout the war. At the new state convention, Smith sought to include all territory west of the Blue Ridge in the new state and locate its capital at White Sulphur Springs. Many in the federal government also wanted Eastern Panhandle counties in the new state so as to include the Baltimore & Ohio Railroad.[18] Smith, however, failed to convince other delegates at the convention to adopt such boundaries.[19]

In about 1861, President Lincoln appointed Colonel Smith to serve as the U.S. Attorney for the Western District of Virginia, soon to be West Virginia. U.S. Senator

---

[17] See Curry, *A House Divided*.
[18] This issue was later addressed and resolved in the Supreme Court case of *Virginia v. West Virginia*, 78 U.S. 39, 20 L.Ed. 67 (1871).
[19] Atkinson, *History of Kanawha County*, 263.

Thomas S. Carlile recommended Smith, in a letter signed by both State Auditor Samuel Crane and State Treasurer Campbell Tarr, urging President Lincoln to appoint Smith because he "is one of the ablest lawyers in this part of the state, comes from the right locality, has held the office under Fillmore's administration, and will accept it now from a sense of duty to his country. No better selection could be made . . . ." At the bottom of Carlile's letter, U.S. Senator Waitman T. Willey added his endorsement, saying "the appointment of Col. Smith will give almost universal satisfaction and add great influence to our moral strength in NW Virginia."[20] Moreover, Atkinson noted Lincoln's Attorney General, Edward Banks, regarded Smith as "one of the ablest of the one hundred or more district attorneys then in the service of the United States." Smith continued as U.S. attorney until about 1867 when he resigned.[21]

Although Colonel Smith remained a staunch Union defender, he nevertheless opposed many federal measures against the South after the Civil War. He aligned with a small minority of pro-Union Democrats who called themselves the "Conservative party" seeking to attract support from unhappy conservative Republicans. Although Smith became a logical choice as Democratic nominee for West Virginia governor in 1866, his campaign resulted in failure:

> Smith launched his main attack against the registration law and the disenfranchising amendment to the state constitution and carried the campaign to remote corners of the state. It was without avail. Though the Conservative party retained some representation in both branches of the legislature, the entire state ticket went down to defeat.

20 *Ibid.*
21 Some historic accounts report that Smith served from 1862-1867, while others say he was appointed in 1861 and resigned in 1868.

Conservatives must have received scant satisfaction from the fact that their candidate for governor [Smith] was defeated by a majority of [only] 6,644 votes in a total of 40,960 votes cast.[22]

Indeed, at that time, so close to the war's end, no Democrat stood a realistic chance of winning statewide election. But Colonel Smith nevertheless served a term in West Virginia's legislature and successfully killed a bill to move the state capital from Charleston. Although Colonel Smith lost his 1866 race for governor, Democratic Party officials approached him to run for governor once more in 1868. Smith "refused emphatically."[23]

Although Colonel Smith supported the Union, his son, Isaac Noyes Smith, served briefly in the Confederate Army just as the war began.[24] This service likely influenced Colonel Smith's work to eliminate test oaths, which prevented his son and others who fought for or sympathized with the Confederacy from practicing law in West Virginia. Though Isaac Smith began practicing with his father in 1852 and was elected to the West Virginia legislature in 1860, his stint in the Confederate Army interrupted his legal practice until the test oath was repealed in 1872.

Isaac's service in the Confederate Army caused grief for both father and son. As Colonel Smith supported West Virginia statehood and maintenance of the Union, Isaac wrote in his journal, "Why my father has chosen to place me in this terrible situation is beyond my

---

[22] Summers, *Johnson Newlon Camden*, 124-125.
[23] Summers, *Johnson Newlon Camden*, 130-131.
[24] Isaac Smith enlisted July 15, 1861 at Charleston, West Virginia, as a private. On that same day he mustered into Company "H" of the 22nd Virginia Infantry. He was promoted to major on August 15, 1861, and resigned on November 6, 1861.

comprehension."[25] Isaac officially resigned from the Confederate Army in November 1861, not four months into his enlistment, because he disliked General John Buchanan Floyd, who accused him of being loyal to the Union. Presumably, those accusations originated in Colonel Smith's Union loyalties.

Colonel Smith was not, however, as hard on the South as were others. For example, he opposed harsh retribution after the war's end and welcomed Confederate sympathizers back into economic life. Perhaps most controversial by today's standards, after his son Isaac's slave escaped to Union lines, Colonel Smith tried to return the slave to the South—despite Col. Smith's opposing slavery, despite his own father's freeing family slaves years earlier, and despite his serving as U.S. attorney while such slave returns were illegal.

Colonel Smith's strong opinions apparently won him both ardent supporters and detractors. According to Gov. Atkinson, Colonel Smith was "not kindly treated by a portion of the people."[26] Historian William Laidley hints at something similar: "We do not know why he was not regarded with favor by some . . . [but] perhaps he . . . expressed his opinions too freely on the subject of slavery or on some political, or church, question, for he never hesitated to speak out, without using any tact or evasion. . . ." Laidley added that Colonel Smith "was of a temperament that made him friends and that also made him unpopular with some. That is, he was outspoken as to his own opinions and firm in his convictions."[27]

---

[25] Ryan Quinn, "250 years of Charleston history, through 4 families," *Charleston Gazette-Mail*, 27 October 2017.

[26] Atkinson, *History of Kanawha County*, 261.

[27] Laidley, *A History of Charleston and Kanawha County*, 287 & 950.

But Colonel Smith was not entirely hard-edged. For instance, a Methodist minister described a temperance gathering: "Before the preacher finished his description, the audience was in tears; some wept aloud. One deep, manly voice sobbed so loud[ly] as to be heard over the whole house. It was the voice of that great-hearted lawyer, Col. Ben Smith."[28] Others noted Colonel Smith did not hold grudges and listened to others' opinions even when his own opinions differed.[29]

Despite his many accomplishments outside the legal profession, Colonel Smith is remembered mainly as one of the country's foremost real estate lawyers. In the words of historian Brooks McCabe, "No single person in West Virginia's history has been as influential in the creation of a legal framework to provide clear titles for land transfers as Benjamin Harrison Smith."[30] Smith approached his cases with common sense and passion, always with the client's interests top of mind.

Over time, Colonel Smith stepped away from his legal practice, turning it over to his son, to focus on his farm on the Kanawha River, about seven miles downstream from Charleston in an area now known as Dunbar.[31] Probably Colonel Smith retired from practicing law entirely after his son, Isaac, died in 1883. Yet, a map of Charleston in 1873 shows the Smith & Knight law offices on Front Street, now Kanawha Boulevard, on the river side between Capitol and Hale streets.[32] Colonel Smith died on December 10, 1887, at age 90 and is buried in the Spring Hill Cemetery in Charleston.

---

28 *West Virginia Historical Magazine*, Vol. 2, No. 1, 52.

29 Atkinson, 264-265; Laidley, 287-288.

30 McCabe, "Benjamin Harrison Smith, Land Titles, and the West Virginia Constitution," 1.

31 *West Virginia Historical Magazine*, Vol. 1, No. 3, 15.

32 Andre and Cohen, *Kanawha Images*, Vol. 2, 27.

Edward Boardman Knight

Edward Boardman Knight likely came to know Colonel Smith through Smith's marriage into the Noyes family (in 1826 he married Roxalana Noyes).[33] The Knight and Noyes families both came to West Virginia from Newbury, Massachusetts; and three Knight daughters married three Noyes sons. Edward Knight and Colonel Smith eventually entered into law practice together in 1864.

Edward Knight was born in 1834.[34] Initially he trained to become a machinist, but by age 21 went to study at New London Literary and Scientific Institute; he graduated from Dartmouth College in 1861. Knight taught briefly at Washington College (now called Washington and Lee University), then studied law with George W. Everett at New London, New Hampshire. He was admitted to the bar in 1863 and practiced briefly in both New London and Dover, New Hampshire; in 1864 Knight accepted "a partnership in an old, established law firm in Charleston, West Virginia, which he accepted, and at once moved to the place . . . ."[35] Thus, his professional union with Colonel Smith gave birth to Smith & Knight law firm in 1864.

[33] Three of John Knight's daughters—Elizabeth, Mary, and Hannah—married three of Nicholas Noyes's sons—Cutting, Timothy, and James—in 1674, 1681, and 1684, respectively.

[34] Edward Boardman Knight was born on August 22, 1834, in Hancock, New Hampshire, as the son of Asa Knight and Melinda Adams Knight. His parents owned a farm in the southwest part of town.

[35] Ramsdell, *The History of Milford*, 346.

The same year Knight partnered with Smith, he married Hannah Elizabeth White of Newport, New Hampshire. They had three children—Edward Wallace, Harold Warren, and Mary Ethel.[36] After Knight's wife died in 1878, he married Mary Elizabeth White, Hannah's sister. Despite spending most of his life in Charleston, Knight often returned to his New England roots; he enjoyed the outdoors, especially fishing, and spent summers in Sunnipee Lake, New Hampshire.

Knight developed a stellar legal reputation—he reportedly possessed an encyclopedic knowledge of the law, a particularly valuable skill when textbooks and encyclopedias were rare. In *Bench and Bar of West Virginia*, Atkinson indicates Knight applied this vast knowledge in winning cases in effective ways. According to Atkinson, Edward Knight had few equals in the legal profession.[37] Colonel Smith's son, Isaac, called Knight "the purest-minded man with the highest moral ideals" he had ever known.[38] Governor William A. MacCorkle recounted this story about Knight:

> I was traveling in northern New York and was riding in the smoking room with a gentleman who had boarded the train at some local station. After a while my companion asked me if I was from the South, and I informed him that I was from West Virginia. He mentioned several people and among others asked if I knew Mr. Knight. I replied, "Yes." He said,

---

[36] Mary Ethel married George W. McClintic, who served for many years as U.S. District Judge in the Southern District of West Virginia.

[37] Atkinson, *Bench and Bar of West Virginia*, 47.

[38] Laidley, 424.

"He is a very great lawyer." I answered, "Yes, he is." He said, "He is a great speaker, has a lot of wit and humor." I agreed with him. He added, "I was there four or five months ago and they were trying a moot case at the Capitol. I was directed to the meeting: I heard that the federal judge was to preside and it was going to be an interesting affair, and I went. Mr. Knight made a great speech. He kind of cleaned up that other lawyer." I said, "Yes, I expect he did." I did not think it necessary to tell him that I was the "other lawyer."

[Mr. Knight's] great forte, however, was in the general trial of a case. In the examination of witnesses, he had very few equals. I remember well that he frequently repeated the last words of the witness; and when the witness answered, he used the expression, "Aha! Aha!" The combination of great knowledge of practice and pleading, ability to cross-examine, splendid oratorical abilities, and great experience as a trial lawyer made him dangerous in any class of case.[39]

Beyond his law practice, Knight served as solicitor for the City of Charleston several years and was a member delegate to the 1872 constitutional convention. Article XIII of the Constitution protected claimants who paid taxes on their land and addressed handling delinquent land taxes. It also restored the right to vote to former Confederates. For the land-title provisions in Article XIII, Knight was

[39] MacCorkle, *Recollections of Fifty Years*, 57.

"principal author of this most important article with its complex and significant ramifications."[40]

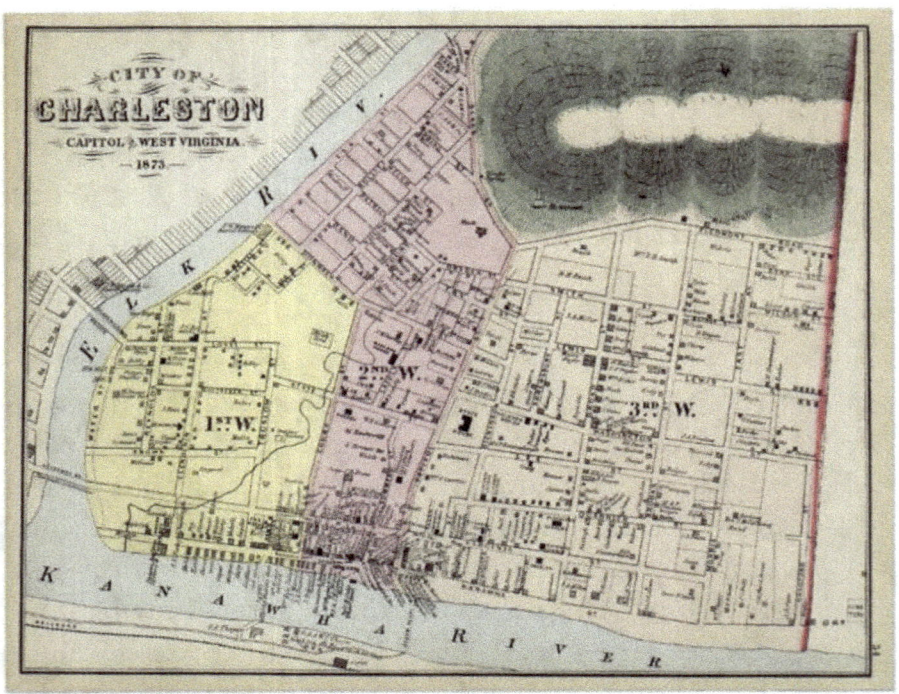

A Charleston map from 1873 shows Smith & Knight law offices on the bank of the Kanawha River, diagonally across Kanawha and Court streets, from the courthouse. Governor MacCorkle described Charleston during the mid-1800s as "a conservative old aristocratic town . . . inhabited largely by one class of people."[41] With the coal-mining industry starting to prosper, false land titles began cropping up, prompting plenty of litigation for lawyers like Smith and Knight. As with his business partner, Colonel

[40] McCabe, *West Virginia History*, "Benjamin Harrison Smith, Land Titles, and the West Virginia Constitution," Spring 2012, 22.
[41] MacCorkle, *Recollections of Fifty Years*, 49.

Smith, political activists began asking Knight to run for office. In 1887, he was considered a candidate for the U.S. Senate.

Upon the death of Colonel Smith's son, Isaac N. Smith (profiled in chapter 3), Knight partnered with George S. Couch, and the firm's name officially changed to Knight & Couch in 1883. Knight and Couch continued practicing together until Knight's retirement in 1892.

Edward Boardman Knight died on December 16, 1897, allegedly with "stomach trouble" that had plagued him for months despite "vigorous and rugged constitution."[42] An obituary said he "ranked among the ablest lawyers of his state and retained his position as long as he remained in the profession." Another news report said Knight's death left "nothing more hurtful to his memory than the earnest respect and the abiding affection of every person who ever came in contact with him."[43] Knight is buried in Spring Hill Cemetery in Charleston.

---

[42] *Wheeling Intelligencer*, December 17, 1897.
[43] *The Daily Gazette*, December 16, 1897.

EDWARD B. KNIGHT TOMBSTONE

Isaac Noyes Smith

Colonel Benjamin Smith's only son, Isaac Noyes Smith, was born in 1831. He graduated from Washington College in 1852 (now called Washington and Lee University), studied law at Judge Brockenbrough's law school, and immediately began practicing with his father. Isaac was elected to the West Virginia legislature in 1860 and married Caroline S. Quarrier that year.

Practicing law and starting a family were not the only things on Isaac's mind at this time. In 1858, following other young locals, he joined Kanawha Riflemen, a militia organized and led by lawyer George S. Patton (grandfather of General George S. Patton of World War II fame). The group drilled, learned military procedures, and studied military tactics. Smith began as a private, but later became an officer. Then, when the Civil War began, the Kanawha Riflemen belonged to the 22nd Virginia Regiment with Isaac second in command, a major.[44]

Smith's brief service in the Confederate Army revealed his difference from his pro-Union father, Benjamin. After the war, test oaths required civil

---

[44] Isaac Smith enlisted on 15 July 1861 at Charleston, West Virginia, as a private. On that same day he mustered into Company "H" of the 22nd Virginia Infantry. He was promoted to major on August 15, 1861, but resigned on November 6, 1861. A fuller history of Isaac's war experiences—including his resignation from the army, conduct during the war, and problems returning to the practice of law—appear in *West Virginia History, A Virginian's Dilemma*, Volume XXVII, April 1966, Number 3.

servants, military officers, and lawyers to swear not only present and future loyalty to the U.S., but also to affirm they had never engaged in disloyal conduct. Such test oaths were repealed in 1872 in part because of advocacy by Isaac's father. Consequently, Isaac Smith began practicing law again, this time with both his father and his father's new partner, Edward Knight.

Although Isaac's presence in the firm arose in large part from his lineage, he nonetheless quickly demonstrated the skills to warrant his employment. At the time in Kanawha County, most important litigation involved

Smith & Knight representing one side or the other. According to Laidley, Isaac "came of an ancestry marked by strong, brave, and able men; and his distinction at the bar was only less than that of his father, who survived him."[45] Governor MacCorkle asserted that though Isaac was not a great courtroom orator, he could still prove eloquent. And even though he paled as a speaker compared to both his father and Edward Knight, Isaac became a premier business lawyer at a crucial moment in Kanawha County's economic growth. Governor MacCorkle notes,

> I was in court in the spring of 1882 when Mr. Isaac N. Smith handed in a decree dismissing and settling the famous old salt case of Dickinson and Shrewsbury. This was the Jarndyce versus Jarndyce of the Kanawha Bar. I remember Mr. Smith's speech concerning this case. It was a very beautiful and touching address. The case had been pending for about sixty years and was a very remarkable piece of litigation. Mr. Smith in glowing language told the court of the great industrial and political changes that had taken place in the world and especially in this country since the institution of that suit—the Mexican War, the great Civil War of our country, the War of 1871, and others. Mr. Charles Hedrick arose and asked that the court appoint a day for formal obsequies of the case. It was set for Saturday following Mr. Smith's statement. I regret that the wonderful and interesting history detailed by the lawyers was not preserved.[46]

In addition, MacCorkle described Isaac as the first business lawyer in the southern West Virginia Bar. He was the first, along with his father-in-law Alexander W. Quarrier, to author a contract for coal mining; the two men

[45] Laidley, *History of Charleston and Kanawha County*, 937.
[46] MacCorkle, *The Recollections of Fifty Years*, 115.

"practically originated the coal lease," an instrument still used in the industry.[47]

In one of his successes, Isaac secured about $2.5 million of Virginia state funding for railroad construction from Covington to the Ohio River. His remarks in the Virginia House of Delegates about the legislation proved so persuasive that the *Richmond Enquirer* published it as a stand-alone pamphlet just before the Civil War.[48]

Isaac and his wife, Caroline Quarrier Smith, had six children. They were long-time members of the local Presbyterian church, and for many years Isaac served as an elder. In 1883 Isaac died at his home in Charleston at age 52, four years before his father died. After Isaac's death, the firm's sole remaining partner, Edward Knight, brought George S. Couch on board; and the firm's name changed to Knight & Couch.

[47] *Ibid.*
[48] *Remarks of Mr. Smith of Kanawha on the Covington and Ohio Rail Road Bill in the House of Delegates of Virginia, Richmond Enquirer,* 1860, West Virginia State Archives.

George S. Couch

George S. Couch was born in Mason County (then Virginia) in 1852.[49] He attended school in Mason County and began college in 1868 in Marietta, Ohio. After graduating in 1872, he studied at Arbuckle on the Kanawha River with his father, a lawyer, until April 1873 and was admitted to the bar the same year. Couch moved to Charleston and, according to William Laidley's *History of Charleston and Kanawha County*, earned a reputation as an able lawyer.

As a lawyer, George Couch began a partnership in 1884 first with Charles Hedrick and then with Edward B. Knight, helping to perpetuate what eventually became Jackson Kelly. According to Laidley, Knight & Couch was the leading law firm in Charleston in the decades following the partnership.

Besides law, Couch engaged in business. For instance, he helped organize Kanawha National Bank in 1881 and served as its president; he was also first president of Charleston National Bank founded in 1884. In real estate, Couch owned a farm west of Charleston in what is now Dunbar; tradition suggests Couch named this town in honor of his friend David Dunbar, a lawyer.

Couch married Laura McMaster, and together they had three children, including George S. Couch Jr., who joined his father's firm in 1905. The family lived within walking distance of the law office on the north side of

---

[49] Couch's ancestor owned several thousand acres in Goochland County, Virginia, along with many slaves, but the family converted to Quakerism and subsequently freed them.

Kanawha River, on the east side of Bradford Street, about a half-mile from the courthouse and city building. Couch Sr., though a Democrat, avoided active participation in politics. He, too, was a member of the Presbyterian church.

In 1892 Edward B. Knight retired from the law, but his son Edward W. Knight continued practicing with the firm. With Couch Sr.'s many business interests requiring his time and with the firm's caseload growing, he decided to step back. Couch Sr. himself retired from the firm in 1897, but later returned to law in a new partnership, with Samuel Flournoy and George Price, which eventually led to the modern law firm Spilman, Thomas & Battle. Couch retired for good in 1905 and died in 1915.

In 1892 Edward W. Knight (son of Edward B. Knight) acquired two new partners, James F. Brown and Malcolm Jackson; and together they changed the firm's name to Brown, Jackson & Knight. George S. Couch Jr. (son of George S. Couch Sr.) soon joined the firm as well. Thus began a momentous period as the firm transitioned to a new generation who guided it into the 20th century.

Brown, Jackson & Knight

The first lawyer listed in the firm's new 1892 name—James Frederick Brown—was a native of Charleston, West Virginia.[50] In 1888, Brown had joined Malcolm Jackson before Brown and Jackson both joined Edward W. Knight (in 1892), giving the firm the name it carried from 1892 to 1947.

Under terms of this new partnership dated December 3, 1891, three different groups came together: (1) Edward B. Knight and George S. Couch; (2) Edward W. Knight; and (3) the law firm of Brown & Jackson, comprising James F. Brown and Malcom Jackson. This agreement meant that Knight & Couch dissolved their business to fold it into the newly named and newly created partnership. Likewise, the law firm Brown & Jackson dissolved to fold into the new entity. Although dated December 1891, the agreement took effect only on January 1, 1892, with all profits and losses shared equally among the parties.

According to former governor George Atkinson, the firm was "known as one of the strongest and ablest in the entire state as well as one of the most successful. They are not only good lawyers, but they are all honorable,

---

[50] James F. Brown was born at The Elms in Charleston, West Virginia, on March 7, 1852, to James Henry Brown and Louisa Mayer Beuhring. His father, James H. Brown, served on the first West Virginia Supreme Court and formed Brown & Brown, later Brown & Jackson, which merged with the Smith & Knight firm into Brown, Jackson & Knight in 1892.

upright gentlemen, who are thoroughly trustworthy and reliable."[51]

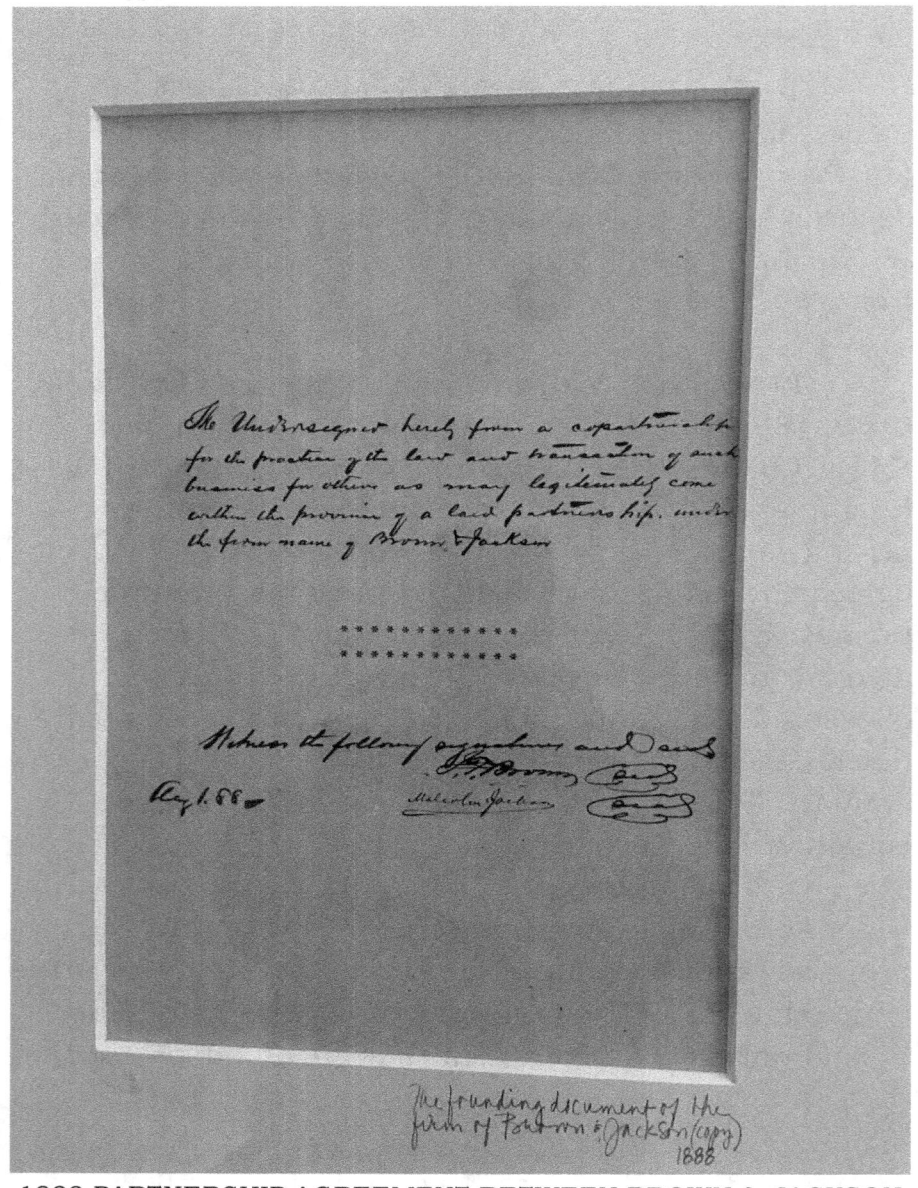

1888 PARTNERSHIP AGREEMENT BETWEEN BROWN & JACKSON

---

[51] Atkinson, *Bench and Bar of West Virginia*, 516.

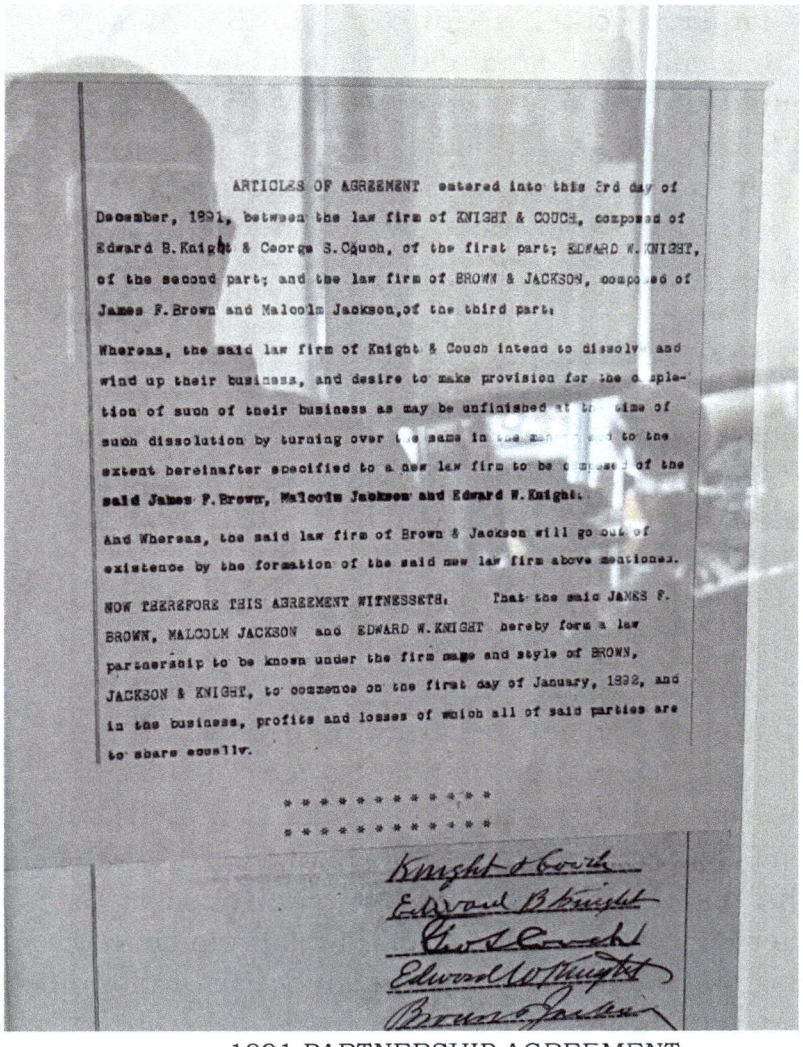

ARTICLES OF AGREEMENT entered into this 3rd day of December, 1891, between the law firm of KNIGHT & COUCH, composed of Edward B. Knight & George S. Couch, of the first part; EDWARD W. KNIGHT, of the second part; and the law firm of BROWN & JACKSON, composed of James F. Brown and Malcolm Jackson, of the third part;

Whereas, the said law firm of Knight & Couch intend to dissolve and wind up their business, and desire to make provision for the completion of such of their business as may be unfinished at the time of such dissolution by turning over the same in the manner and to the extent hereinafter specified to a new law firm to be composed of the said James F. Brown, Malcolm Jackson and Edward W. Knight.

And Whereas, the said law firm of Brown & Jackson will go out of existence by the formation of the said new law firm above mentioned.

NOW THEREFORE THIS AGREEMENT WITNESSETH: That the said JAMES F. BROWN, MALCOLM JACKSON and EDWARD W. KNIGHT hereby form a law partnership to be known under the firm name and style of BROWN, JACKSON & KNIGHT, to commence on the first day of January, 1892, and in the business, profits and losses of which all of said parties are to share equally.

* * * * * * * * * * *
* * * * * * * * * * *

1891 PARTNERSHIP AGREEMENT

James F. Brown

Brown graduated in 1873 from West Virginia University and subsequently earned a master's degree (1875) and an LL.D. (1917). After studying with his father, Brown was admitted to the bar in 1875 and practiced with his father, together creating the firm Brown & Brown. Specializing in land and corporate law, their firm represented many companies involved in the growing coal industry such as Norfolk and Western Railway. Brown gained a reputation as an able attorney with "few equals, and perhaps no superiors, among the members of the West Virginia Bar."[52]

In 1888, after his father retired, Brown merged first with Malcom Jackson (discussed below) and then in 1892 with Edward W. Knight (also discussed below) to form Brown, Jackson & Knight, which soon became West Virginia's leading law firm.

As senior member of the firm, Brown argued cases for many clients in front of various appeals courts. On two occasions, he argued in front of the United States Supreme Court. The first (technically three separate dockets) was *King v. West Virginia and Spruce Coal & Lumber Company; King v. West Virginia, Egbert, Trustee, et al.*; and King v. West Virginia, U.B. Buskirk, Trustee, et al. This dispute involved tracts of land seized by the state after Henry King failed to list the land in county land books. Thereafter, Brown's client, a coal and lumber company, purchased one of the tracts from a state trustee. When King attempted to retrieve the lands, a Marion County court ruled against him. After unsuccessfully appealing to the West Virginia Supreme Court, King brought the case before the U.S. Supreme Court, which upheld the lower court rulings.

---

[52] Atkinson, *Bench and Bar of West Virginia*, 186.

In addition, Brown was active in West Virginia politics. He began his career in 1883 when elected (with his father) to the House of Delegates from Kanawha County. As an influential member of the Judicial and Financial committees, he maneuvered bills through the House that reflected his clients' interests. For example, he wrote and guided House Bill 60, which allowed Coal River Railroad Company to connect with the Chesapeake & Ohio line. In 1890, Governor Emmanuel Wilson appointed Brown to the State University Board of Regents, where Brown served under four subsequent governors, despite their sometimes-differing political opinions. Meanwhile, he served on the Charleston city council for 20 years.

Brown's work was vital to the commercial life of Charleston and the Kanawha Valley. In banking, he was vice president and director of Kanawha Valley Bank and was a charter member of Central Trust Company. Furthermore, Brown served as a trustee of Charleston General Hospital, the first large facility of its kind in the city, and as vice president of George Washington Life Insurance Company.

Brown married Jennie Woodbridge and had six children, including Benjamin, a member of Brown, Jackson & Knight until 1945. Brown, too, attended Kanawha Presbyterian Church. He died in 1921 and is buried in Charleston's Spring Hill Cemetery. His legacy included a law firm moving toward high stature in the state.

Malcolm Jackson

Malcom Jackson, who gave the firm its most prominent modern name, was born in 1860 in Richmond, Indiana, and studied at Earlham College (Indiana). Thereafter he attended the U.S. Naval Academy and graduated in 1881 from the University of Virginia law school.

Jackson began practicing law in Charleston in 1881 and established himself as a brilliant advocate "particularly able in courthouse trials."[53] By 1888, Jackson attracted the attention of James F. Brown, a leading attorney in the area, and they formed the law firm Brown & Jackson. Four years later, they merged with Edward W. Knight to form Brown, Jackson & Knight.

As Brown, Jackson, and Knight, the firm earned a strong reputation as excellent representatives of various coal companies. One prominent case was *Norfolk & Western Railway Company v. Fort Dearborn Coal & Export Company*.[54] Jackson's client, the coal company, had purchased 897 tons of coal from another company to transport to tidewater Virginia for export by the railway company. But without the coal company's consent, the railroad confiscated the coal en route for use as fuel. When the coal company sued for recovery of lost income, the trial court ruled against the railroad, which appealed because the trial judge disallowed testimony that would have resulted in a smaller judgment. Consequently, the

---

[53] Atkinson, *Bench and Bar of West Virginia,* 250.
[54] 287 U.S. 134 (1932).

appeals court overturned the trial court and sent the case back. With the previously excluded testimony then included, the new trial ended like the first; but because so much time had elapsed, accrued interest increased the damage award by almost $1,000.

Jackson was active in politics beginning in 1896 when, appointed by Governor Atkinson, he became law officer of the West Virginia National Guard, a post which granted him the rank of brigadier general. In 1901, he won election to the House of Delegates, where he served on the Federal Relations Committee and chaired the Judiciary Committee. Jackson proposed several bills though none of them ultimately became law. One proposal, House Bill 15, called for creation of a State Board of Arbitration and Conciliation to settle labor disputes. Another, House Bill 152, would have required the state to pay lawyers when a court ordered them to represent indigent persons.

In 1922, Jackson retired from the law, but remained active in civic life. He served as communicant in the Protestant Episcopal Church. He married Louise Brown and had two children, including Thomas, who followed his father into the firm. Malcolm Jackson died in 1931 from injuries suffered in a car accident while visiting friends in New York City.

Edward W. Knight

Edward W. Knight was born in Charleston in 1866 to Edward B. Knight and his wife Roxalana. He graduated from his father's alma mater, Dartmouth, in 1887, then returned to Charleston to study law at Knight & Couch. In 1889 he was admitted to the bar and became a member of the firm. Three years later, Knight became a founding partner of Brown, Jackson & Knight.

During his career Knight specialized in corporate law, a field "in which he became unusually familiar and successful."[55] His skill led to special relationships with clients such as the Deepwater, Tidewater, and Virginia Railroads Company, for whom he served as general counsel for 27 years, and the Virginian Railway Company, for whom he served as general counsel. Moreover, Knight was associate chairman of the West Virginia Railroad Association. Unfortunately, his reputation embroiled him in one of the most bitter labor disputes of his time.

In the early 20th century, the United Mine Workers Association (UMWA) began to advance into West Virginia's coal fields. But their attempts to unionize workers often met with bitter resistance from coal operators. The union achieved moderate success, however, especially in the Kanawha Valley, where in 1902 it received grudging recognition among coal operators. Although the Paint Creek area of the valley, about 20 miles east of Charleston, became unionized, on April 1, 1912, the miners' contract expired. When approached by the UMWA with a list of demands for the new contract, coal operators refused to consent and withdrew recognition of the union. The miners and UMWA soon declared a strike.

---

[55] Atkinson, *Bench and Bar of West Virginia*, 242.

EDWARD W. KNIGHT
(second from right on the ground)

Most demands for a settlement involved union issues. Miners demanded the right to organize, to end company blacklisting of employees who join the UMWA, and to trade at non-company stores. Tempers flared, and both sides settled in for a long struggle. Operators brought in agents from the Baldwin-Felts detective agency in Beckley to act as mine guards and to evict striking miners from their company-owned homes. Strikers then set up tent cities along various roads and railroads. Some brought guns into these camps, and many clashes between guards and miners ensued, some resulting in deaths. With civil authorities unable to end the rising violence, Governor William Glascock declared martial law and sent in the state militia to restore order. In November 1912 he appointed a special commission to study and resolve the situation. When that commission recommended that the company stop blacklisting workers and endorsed the right of labor to organize, the strike nevertheless continued, with martial law in effect sporadically, until May 1913 when new Governor Henry Hatfield imposed a settlement. It allowed miners to organize and to trade at non-company stores, and it imposed a nine-hour workday.

Later that year, the U.S. Senate formed a committee to investigate the strike, which had gained national attention. Knight, whose clients included some of the coal operators involved, along with Zachary Vinson, who represented some other coal companies, wrote both a preliminary statement and a brief on behalf of the operators. In the preliminary statement, operators laid blame for the strike and ensuing violence entirely on the UMWA.

The union, Knight and Vinson asserted, sought to control the entire North American coal industry, and their sole desire in organizing West Virginia was "increasing the cost of mining in the State to such a figure as to shut out West Virginia competition" for the Midwestern coal states. The miners of Paint Creek, these operators contended, were satisfied with their working conditions, stating that "not more than ten percent of the men leaving the employment of these companies, ceased to work voluntarily." The coal companies charged, too, that the UMWA brought representatives into the area who made "the most incendiary speeches, openly counselling assault and murder."[56]

Knight never ventured far into the political arena. He held only one office, a position on the common council of Charleston from 1891 to 1894. Instead, he devoted his energies to commercial pursuits. Knight served as director for several companies, including Kanawha Valley Bank, Virginian Railway Company, Central Trust Company, Virginian Electric Incorporated, Trust Company of Norfolk, and the National Bank of Commerce. And he devoted time to his alma mater as a Dartmouth trustee from 1925 to 1935.

Knight married Mary Dana with whom he had three children. He never retired and remained an active partner in the firm when he died in 1939.

Valentine L. Black

Valentine L. Black was born in Beaver County, Pennsylvania, in 1865 and moved to Charleston when only seven years old. He became interested in law and studied under his older brother, H. K. Black, a Kanawha County circuit judge. In 1896 Black was admitted to the bar, and one year later he joined Brown, Jackson & Knight.

Black handled many prominent cases in his career, including *Kirk v. West Virginia Colliery Company*, a 1914 case before the West Virginia Circuit Court of Appeals, in

---

[56] Rice, *West Virginia: A History*, 224-226.

which Black defended the company against a woman who sought compensation for injury when a stray piece of coal struck her leg as she walked on a railroad track parallel to the coal company. The court ruled her injury resulted from a "very peculiar, unusual, and unexpected occurrence, which no precaution in ordinary reason and experience could have contemplated or forestalled"; therefore the company was not liable. Another case, *Hocking Valley Railway Company v. Lackawanna Coal & Lumber Company*, involved a dispute over transport costs for shipping coal on the railroad operated by Black's client. The railroad eventually won.

Black married Maybell Burdett and had two children. He belonged to the Episcopal church and remained an active member of the firm until his death in 1938.

Leonidas "Lon" H. Kelly

Lon H. Kelly was born in Sutton, West Virginia, in 1871. During his teens, he held various jobs to save money for law school; his jobs included teaching in a public school in nearby Frametown, editing and publishing a newspaper (the *Elk River Progress*), and serving as Braxton County clerk and deputy circuit clerk at the same time.

With his earnings Kelly enrolled at Washington and Lee University and graduated in 1893. That same year he was admitted to the bar in Braxton County. Though Kelly entered private practice in Sutton with William E. Hines, he spent considerable time serving the public. In 1897, for instance, he became Braxton County prosecuting attorney, a position he held until 1900. When his formidable talents caught President Woodrow Wilson's attention, in 1916 Kelly became Assistant U.S. Attorney for the Southern District of West Virginia. The following year, he became District Attorney for the Southern District, a position he held until 1922. During his tenure in that office, Kelly moved to Charleston. And in 1925, after his term as district attorney, Kelly joined Brown, Jackson & Knight.

Beginning in his early years, Kelly was involved in politics. According to one story, on election day 1884 when a man went to the Braxton County Courthouse to see if "the good news was true" (that Grover Cleveland won the presidency), all he found was a 13-year-old Kelly celebrating by standing on his head. Kelly began to hold political office at age 25 when elected mayor of Sutton in 1896. But he only served one year before his election as prosecuting attorney. In 1914, he served as secretary of the state Democratic executive committee, and in 1921 he chaired the Law and Order Committee of Kanawha County. Despite Kelly gaining the Democratic nomination to the state Supreme Court, he lost in the general election. In addition to these public offices, he served as president of two legal organizations, the Charleston Bar Association (1925) and the West Virginia Bar Association (1935).

Kelly was married with three children and belonged to the Presbyterian church. He remained a partner with Brown, Jackson & Knight until his death in 1938. His son Robert followed him into the firm and in 1947 became the first Kelly in the firm's name.

Harold A. Ritz

Harold A. Ritz was born in Wheeling in 1873. After graduation from Marshall University, he moved to Bluefield where he was admitted to the bar in 1894. Ritz quickly entered the political arena and became a circuit-court judge in Mercer County. In 1909, President Taft appointed him U.S. District Attorney for the Southern District of West Virginia, and Ritz served in that position until 1916, when elected justice of the West Virginia Supreme Court.

In 1922, two years before his term on the bench expired, Ritz resigned to become a partner with Brown, Jackson, & Knight. While with the firm, he specialized in corporate law, including railroad and land cases. He left the firm in 1925 to become general counsel for United Fuel Gas Company.

Angus W. McDonald

Angus W. McDonald was born in Louisville in 1878 and graduated from West Virginia University and then the University of Kentucky law school in 1889, the same year he was admitted to the bar in Louisville.

In 1901 McDonald moved to Charleston and joined Brown, Jackson & Knight. In addition to his legal career, McDonald served in the House of Delegates in 1917. He served on the Judiciary and Mining committees and chaired the Railroad Committee. He also acted as president of Provident Life and Casualty Company.

McDonald was married to Elizabeth Brown, daughter of Brown, Jackson & Knight founder James F. Brown. He became a partner in 1911 and left the firm in 1932.

George S. Couch Jr.

George S. Couch, Jr. was born in Charleston in 1880, son of prominent attorney George S. Couch Sr. He earned an undergraduate degree at Princeton University in 1903 and a law degree from University of Virginia in 1905, the same year he began work for Brown, Jackson & Knight.

In his own practice, along with the rest of the firm, Couch specialized in corporate law. For example, in *Farris v. Cabin Creek Consolidated Coal Company* and *Sunday Creek Company v. Gray*, Couch argued successfully in a federal appeals court to protect both companies from civil liability. In *Stewart v. Kelly Axe Manufacturing Company*, he helped write the brief in a case involved an out-of-touch stockholder who sought relief because the company had been sold several times, even though he had not attended a stockholder's meeting in 20 years. Perhaps Couch's most interesting case dealt involved a woman trying to collect on her son's life insurance policy. In *Tabor v. Mutual Life Insurance Company*, Rosa Tabor sued the insurance company (Couch's client), for refusing to pay the claim because they believed Clifton Tabor committed suicide; he shot himself twice in the chest. Several witnesses, however, asserted it was an accident although Taber had asked at least one of them to shoot him. An appellate court sent the case back to the trial court because the trial judge had improperly taken the question of suicide out of the jury's hands.

Couch was married to Ruth Keith Niles Fontaine, but they had no children; he was a member of Kanawha Presbyterian Church. He became a partner with Brown, Jackson & Knight in 1911 and stayed with the firm until his death in 1936.

Couch's death proved controversial in West Virginia: he died after a car crash with a local barber caused his head to hit the pavement—Couch never recovered consciousness. That local barber was charged with manslaughter—the two had feuded before the crash. The source of that feud remains a mystery.

Benjamin B. Brown

Benjamin B. Brown was born in Charleston in 1893, son of James F. Brown. He graduated from Princeton University in 1914 and Harvard Law School in 1917. In 1919, he was admitted to the bar and joined his father's firm a year later, becoming a partner at Brown, Jackson & Knight in 1922.

Brown spent two years after Harvard serving with the U.S. Expeditionary Force in France as a Marine battalion quartermaster. He used his experiences there when elected to the House of Delegates in 1925 and serving as chairman of the Military Affairs Committee. In that role Brown helped steer through a bill that brought laws regarding the West Virginia National Guard into step with those of other states. In addition, he proposed legislation, ultimately unsuccessful, to incorporate the town of Clendenin.

In addition to his political activities, Brown was active in local commercial life. He served on the board of directors of Kanawha Valley Bank, Central Trust Company, Scotia Coal & Coke Company, and Eagle Land Company; he was also president of Lewis Land & Coal Company. Brown belonged to the Kanawha Presbyterian Church where he was both elder and property trustee.

Brown was married to Hester Newhall and had four children. He left Brown, Jackson & Knight in 1947 to create his own practice, but he died after an illness just two years later.

Transition to Modernity—1950s, 1960s, and 1970s

After World War II, the firm began to modernize with the rest of the country and expanded its roll of attorneys. Former state senator John C. Morrison (1901-1974), who first joined the firm in 1925, eventually became a partner and prompted a name change in about 1947 to Jackson, Kelly, Morrison & Moxley.

Along with Morrison, Homer A. Holt joined the firm in 1925. In 1932 at age 34, he became the youngest attorney general in the state's history and then served as governor of West Virginia from 1937 to 1941. Thereafter Holt worked again with the firm, then moved to New York City, then returned to West Virginia in 1953 to join the firm again. That year, 1953, Morrison left to create his own practice, which prompted another name change—to Jackson, Kelly, Holt & Moxley.

From about 1956 onward, the firm was generally known as Jackson Kelly, although the full name read Jackson, Kelly, Holt & O'Farrell, using these well-known names:

- Thomas B. Jackson (1892-1966), member 1922-1966
- Robert G. Kelly (1898-1979), member 1931-1979
- Homer A. Holt (1898-1975), member 1941-1946 & 1953-1975

- William T. O'Farrell (1906-1983), member 1939-1983

Considered large by West Virginia standards, the firm grew to 14 lawyers in 1956 whereupon many Charlestonians called it "We the People."

GOV. HOMER A. HOLT

In 1955 the firm hired James K. Brown, most likely its first ever summer clerk. Summer clerks became increasingly common, though, in the middle-to-late 1960s as did more orderly discussion with associates about their progress. These talks eventually gave birth to the Associates Committee. Before that committee's formation, some partner simply told an associate he was not a candidate for partner, and that was that.

THE ENTIRE FIRM IN 1954
(JACKSON, KELLY, MORRISON & MOXLEY)

In the same ancient tradition used by its founders in the early 1960s, the firm offered young summer students their choice of rent money for the summer or a set of the West Virginia Code—in lieu of salary. Then, in 1967, the firm hired two summer clerks and paid them $200 a month. Summer clerks researched and drafted documents for senior attorneys, but also occasionally filled in for receptionist Mary Jane Hoffman (mother of future lawyer Pete Hoffman).

HOLT AND KELLY AT WORK

As the 1960s ended, "We the People" employed nearly 20 lawyers, all headquartered on the 16th floor of Kanawha Valley Building next to the Diamond Department Store on Charleston's bustling main thoroughfare, Capitol Street. The firm's furnishings were tasteful, but generally understated, reflecting the partners' prevailing view that clients did not want to think they paid for their lawyers' elegant surroundings.

KANAWHA VALLEY BUILDING
(firm offices unti 1977)

1960S (ABOVE) AND 1970S (BELOW)

In the early 1970s, as the state's then oldest and largest law firm, Jackson Kelly still operated as it and others had done in the past. For example, Saturday served as a workday with a receptionist on duty. Depositions often occurred on those Saturdays to accommodate witnesses. Staff made originals and carbon copies without electronic assistance. Large projects such as injunctions required many copies, sometimes made with mimeograph machines which gave the paper a distinctive smell. Cigarette smoke pervaded the rooms.

Of course, paper governed most days—paper files, paper discovery, and paper communications. Paper everywhere. The firm's law library—books and papers—offered critical research tools. Information flow hinged on paper, though by today's standards that flow was slow, cumbersome, and sometimes unreliable.

EARLY FIRM COMPUTERS

Eventually, typewriter technology advanced with magnetic strips allowing multiple copies at a time. Fax machines came soon, as did copy machines. By the early 1980s, a room-sized Wang computer signified huge changes in legal practice. Although Jackson Kelly remained an old firm, its leaders adeptly adjusted to the latest technologies.

This period meant rapid expansion for the practice. More and more associates joined the firm. In its first 151 years of existence (1822 to 1973), only 66 lawyers worked with Jackson Kelly. But in the next 36 years (1973 to 2009), that number increased by 490 more lawyers.

Such growth required greater focus on attorney recruitment and development, particularly among summer clerks and new associates. The senior associate, called the Bull Associate, served as official liaison between associates and partners. Despite their differences—some partners were fanatical billers, some were very social, and some were scholars—for the most part, senior partners took an interest in clerk and associate welfare. They wanted to signal that everyone had a stake in the firm: once a month, partners invited associates to the weekly partner lunch. And once a year, all partners, associates, former partners, and former associates gathered for a night of revelry at a local country club.

Although firm attorneys certainly worked hard (including on Saturdays), socializing remained important. On Friday mornings, the firm provided donuts; on Friday afternoons partners, associates, paralegals, and others all congregated at a local watering hole to talk shop and tell war stories. Sunday afternoons in the fall they played touch football; in winter they watched basketball.

As it embraced technology, so also the firm embraced social change—hiring Peggy O'Neal, its first female associate, in 1976. Women eventually rose to top management positions, leading to national recognition for the firm's diverse leadership. In 2012, Jackson Kelly was one of only five among the 250 largest firms in the United States where women constituted more than 25 percent of equity partners.[57] Indeed, the firm's CEO during its bicentennial, Ellen Cappellanti, received the first WV Living Wonder Women Justice League Award for Mentorship, testimony to Jackson Kelly's commitment to serve as role models for young men and young women.

But these years of success also marked the passing of several towering figures from the firm's early history. Thomas B. Jackson, a member since 1922, died in 1966; former governor Homer Holt died in 1975. Robert G. Kelly—often called R. G. Kelly—died in 1979. He joined the firm in 1931 and remained a prominent leader throughout its post-war growth. In 1975, he was selected the outstanding coal lawyer at the National Coal Association's Coal Lawyers Conference. Kelly served on many significant corporate and non-profit boards and as state chairman of the Democratic Party; in 1940 he was a delegate-at-large to the Democratic National Convention. Kelly served two terms as president of the West Virginia Chamber of Commerce and three terms as a director of the U.S. Chamber of Commerce.

William T. O'Farrell, a member since 1939, died in 1983—the last partner in the firm's modern name to die. O'Farrell was a leading litigator of his day. In addition to over 90 insurance companies represented in the 1970s, during his career he was involved in most major litigation in West Virginia. O'Farrell was renowned in the rough and tumble of litigation practice as a true gentleman who usually referred to lawyers as "squire."

---

[57] Staci Zaretsky, "Which Biglaw Firms Actually Make Women Equity Partners?" *Above the Law*, 14 July 2012.

CHRISTMAS EVE GATHERING AT ONE VALLEY BUILDING (1977)

A National Firm: 1980s to Present

By the 1980s the firm outgrew its earlier footprint in Charleston and moved a block away into the new One Valley Bank building. In 1985, it moved again, to Laidley Tower.

TRUIST BUILDING
(formerly One Valley Bank and BB&T)

After R. G. Kelly's death in 1979, Andrew L. Blair became the managing partner and the firm hired a true executive director and personnel director. In 1982, the firm expanded outside Charleston by adding a Morgantown office. In common parlance, the firm's name shortened to versions of Jackson Kelly as expansions continued nationwide, creating a firm brand far greater than merely a Charleston group.

FIRM DINNER AT EDGEWOOD COUNTRY CLUB
CIRCA 1982

In 1985, Jackson Kelly expanded into Kentucky by merging with Williams & Palmore, which at the time had offices in Lexington, Louisville, and Owensboro; both firms focused on serving energy-related clients. For a while, the firm operated in Kentucky as Jackson, Kelly, Williams & Palmore, but retained the original name in West Virginia. As a result of the merger in 1985, 85 lawyers worked for the firm—42 partners and 43 associates—with plans to hire 13 more that year. The merger also meant the firm operated in five cities— Charleston and Morgantown in West Virginia; Lexington, Louisville, and Owensboro in Kentucky. But the Owensboro office closed on December 31, 1985, and a new office opened in Frankfurt, Kentucky, on May 1, 1987. The firm's Louisville attorneys eventually withdrew, leading to that office's closure on January 1, 1988, and in April 1994 the Frankfort office closed and consolidated with the Lexington office.

FIRM LETTERHEAD FROM 1987

On January 1, 1988, the firm ceased using separate names in Kentucky and West Virginia and began uniformly operating as Jackson & Kelly in recognition of two families who provided a number of outstanding partners for over a century.

LAIDLEY (NOW TRUIST) TOWER

On June 1, 1989, the Martinsburg, West Virginia, firm Wm. Richard McCune, L.C., and the New Martinsville, West Virginia, firm Brennan & Francis joined Jackson & Kelly and continued to practice law under the last name. Less than a year later, in February 1990, the firm opened offices in Washington, D.C.; in July 1993 in Denver, Colorado (discussed more below); also in July 1993 in Clarksburg, West Virginia. Additional offices opened in Parkersburg, West Virginia, in June 1995 and Fairmont, West Virginia, in June 1996; when the latter office opened, the Clarksburg office closed. In March 1997, the firm opened a new office in Wheeling, West Virginia; that same month, the Charles Town, West Virginia, office closed.

In 1993, Jackson Kelly attorney Laura Beverage founded the firm's first office west of the Mississippi River in Denver, Colorado; it remains the firm's outpost farthest from headquarters in Charleston. The firm's strong roots in mining and workplace safety brought it to Denver, where attorneys represented international metal mines for copper, gold, silver, palladium, molybdenum, lithium, uranium, and rare earth minerals. Since its opening, the Denver office has diversified from mining and occupational safety to include litigation, medical malpractice, employment, business transactions, and government relations.

Effective January 1, 1999, Jackson & Kelly, a general partnership, converted to Jackson & Kelly PLLC, a West Virginia professional limited liability company.

Then, on September 16, 2002, the firm dropped its ampersand and is now Jackson Kelly PLLC. That year Jackson Kelly became the first law firm in West Virginia to establish ancillary businesses, Jackson Kelly Solutions LLC, providing business and environmental consulting.

After re-establishing the Clarksburg, West Virginia, office in 2003, the firm consolidated its Fairmont office with Clarksburg in 2004. And in 2004, Jackson Kelly opened a Pittsburgh, Pennsylvania, office, but closed offices in Parkersburg, West Virginia, in 2006 and New Martinsville, West Virginia, in 2008. Finally, the firm relocated the Clarksburg office to Bridgeport, West Virginia, in 2015.

On May 1, 2012, Jackson Kelly added the energy boutique firm Gormley Gormley & Yuhas (based in Indiana, Pennsylvania) to its Pittsburgh office, bringing that office to 14 lawyers at that time. That summer the firm opened an office in Canton, Pennsylvania, though it subsequently consolidated into the Pittsburgh office.

On June 12, 2012, Jackson Kelly opened an office in Canton, Ohio, to expand its geographic footprint and to accommodate a growing energy practice. That office relocated to Akron, Ohio, in 2014.

Furthermore, the firm continued westward expansion. It opened an Indianapolis office in July 2010 (which subsequently closed) and an Evansville, Indiana, office in June 2011 with a small group of attorneys to serve a growing energy practice, particularly with coal businesses in the Illinois Basin. Effective July 1, 2014, that small Evansville office merged with the 20-attorney firm Rudolph Fine Porter & Johnson (RFPJ), founded in 1987. Unlike most other Jackson Kelly expansions, the RFPJ merger was driven not by energy and mining, but instead by a growing desire to diversify clientele. The RFPJ merger included, too, an office in Crawfordsville, Indiana, and an ancillary business, Lockyear Title, LLC. The Evansville office provides diverse services such as corporate transactional work, litigation, mediation, estate planning and administration, health care, banking, employment, real estate law, municipal law, and intellectual property.

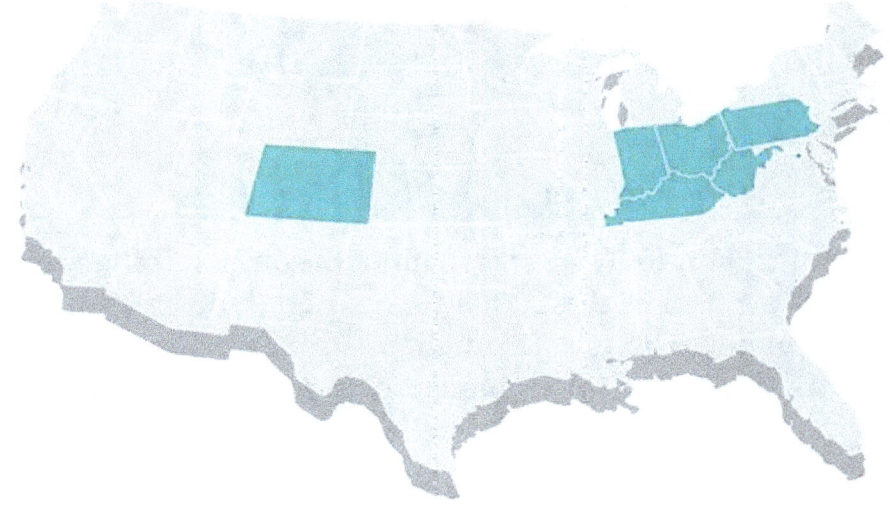

Jackson Kelly rose to national prominence in several important ways. *U.S. News & World Report* consistently recognizes Jackson Kelly as the nation's top firm in mining law, the first law firm to receive that national designation.[58] Moreover, Jackson Kelly ranked number one in the U.S. for workers' compensation practice according to *Woodward and White*'s "Best Lawyers in America." In fact, at various points in time Jackson Kelly has had more lawyers listed in "Best Lawyers" than any other firm in the country. Individual lawyers at the firm garner prominence as well, including two National Coal Lawyers of the Year awards and multiple federal judges at district and circuit levels.

Jackson Kelly has transitioned from a mining and energy law firm in the 1900s to a national, diverse, collegial legal powerhouse. Throughout its origins and growth, Jackson Kelly remained committed to excellent

---

[58] The firm received this designation in 2019, 2017, 2015, 2012, and 2011, among others.

legal work and service to clients. Firm management has long recognized that commitment through collaborative teamwork regardless of rank or pride. The same values that spurred Jackson Kelly from the 19th to the 21st century will help it meet future challenges in an increasingly competitive, global marketplace.

NEW FIRM BRANDING UNVEILED IN 2018

Selected Bibliography

Ambler, Charles H. *West Virginia: The Mountain State.* New York: Prentice-Hall, Inc., 1940.

Andre, Richard and Stan Cohen. *Kanawha County Images*, Vol. II. Charleston, West Virginia: Pictorial Histories Publishing Company Inc., 2001.

Atkinson, George W. *History of Kanawha County from its Organization in 1789 until the Present Time.* Charleston: Office of the West Virginia Journal, 1876.

Atkinson, George W. *Bench and Bar of West Virginia*, 1919. Reprint, General-Books, 2009.

Brinkley, Alan. *The Unfinished Nation: A Concise History of the American People*, Vol. 1, To 1877. 3d ed. New York: McGraw-Hill, 2000.

Contosta, David R. *Lancaster, Ohio 1800-2000: Frontier Town to Edge City.* Columbus: Ohio State University Press, 1999.

Curry, Richard Orr. *A House Divided: A Study of Statehood Politics and Copperhead Movement in West Virginia.* Pittsburgh: University of Pittsburgh Press, 1964.

Hoover, Thomas Nathanael. *The History of Ohio University.* Athens: Ohio University Press, 1954.

Laidley, William S. *History of Charleston and Kanawha County and Representative Citizens*. Chicago: Richmond Arnold Publishing Company, 1911.

MacCorkle, William A. *Recollections of Fifty Years*. New York: G.P. Putnam & Sons, 1928.

Maxwell, William B. III. "Benjamin Harrison Smith and the Quieting of West Virginia's Land Titles." Unpublished manuscript.

McCabe, Brooks F. "Benjamin Harrison Smith, Land Titles, and the West Virginia Constitution." *West Virginia History* 6, no. 1 (2012): 1–34, available at http://www.jstor.org/stable/43264911.

Miller, Paul Ingersoll, "Thomas Ewing: Last of the Whigs." Dissertation, Ohio State University, 1933.

Ramsdell, George A., and William P. Colburn. *The History of Milford*. Concord, N.H.: The Rumford Press, 1901.

Rice, Otis K. *West Virginia: A History*. Lexington, KY: University of Kentucky, 1985.

Shaffer, John W. *Clash of Loyalties*. Morgantown: West Virginia University Press, 2003.

Smith, Christopher. *From the Shenandoah to the Kanawha: The Story of Colonel John Smith, His*

Descendants and Their Ancestors. Charleston: Chris Smith Publishing, 2008.

Summers, Festus P. *Johnson Newlon Camden: A Study in Individualism*. New York: G.P. Putnam & Sons, 1937